NEW POEMS

by Peter Ganick

LUNA BISONTE PRODS
2016

OTHER BOOKS BY PETER GANICK
PUBLISHED BY LUNA BISONTE PRODS

2014
nth client satyr

2012
Remove A Concept Volume 13

2012
orientation

2011
untitled poems for a wednesday evening.

NEW POEMS

The author wishes to thank the editors of the blogs
where some of these poems have appeared.

Editing and book design: C. Mehrl Bennett

ISBN 978-1-938521-29-4

LUNA BISONTE PRODS
137 Leland Ave
Columbus OH 43214-7505 USA

http://www.lulu.com/spotlight/lunabisonteprods

NEW POEMS ONE
Summer 2015

new poem 1.1 |

held, helio presume. goer.
parnassus. which endlessness.
which ends somewhere. for once.
absent. which 'why' applies?
gratias multiflora. meaning nothing.
quota. perhaps immanent—perhaps not.
dardanelles--crossing of which where?
deploy is carnival--temporal temporary—
resists inert issue allocates.
duckpin blotted humanitizing elocution-mopping algae
the function for which...
aisles opt melded & hundreded lapidary converts wait, waiting.
so much waiting radio gleam—
cluttered gallon huddles.
reductions whither blunt arrangements one at a time.
time which was absence—or absent.
can't decide.
if it's necessary to decide then some will.
correctives await in the referrals.
the referrals go nowhere.
a ghostly paradox is resolved of itself.
on its own...
there is absolution of correction...
the correctives red-shift elsewhere.

new poem 1.2 |

it is so utterly quiet. sky flails, publicly.
recurring dross. old
scholar. commence. priors.
those flurrying about. contrasts
with artists.
an opportunistic glance. worrisome.
go nowhere. noes amidst fullness.
while stunted. capable. incapable.
reactionary decision.
which mod arrival? entity.
illbient and concrete.
flounder on toast.

new poem 1.3 |

each rolling history. thematic so it describes.
of pairings in detail. combinations define. motions inscribe.
the telling & stately. which evidence...
portions where?
they're alternatively hungry.
is no use. though it indicates.
omnibus. those that rest.
motions are inserted where details inscribe.
no other.

new poem 1.4 |

relative to.
that of. willing.
not.
happens.
though.
an nth precedent.
tied to.
otherwise.
matching too.

then a crane flies by.
met on a network.
somewhat somewhere.
no knowledge though able.
hat-trick.
none that flee.
imperative.
defensively paradoxical & storage.
endless summer.
detente therefore itself.

new poem 1.6 |

...commences then. at that point.
molecule. infinitives in tryst.
collecting the whole. the precedent is none.
a near miss while driveway. contraption wholly bungled.
coinciding. see what?
they rollover seeing an implausible routine.
scumble. prosody's contact. beset with grommet's willingness.
a somatic voiceover, breathy. in a chorus, a document, 'a' follows 'b'. ach! that's not it. is it. they are then's some.
swerve the route plies. cumbersome triffid waddles. naming holding imperative.
met with high-fives. nods portals. standing in a stadium.
stadia.
compendia behave between beleaguerment. a persuasion wills nothing less.
zero pessimist.

new poem 1.7 |

optimum sound. encroach. non-trial offer.
while reflection opts we mill on a some amalgam.
there's torpor while silent. strike while hot.
silence. rain on an aperture.
opening a can of seltzer. vignettes, not vinegarettes..
plausible in hover-drive so recondite.
naive & similar.

many effects switch the willing cases, blasted comatose.
a signal to refrain & sort.
so non-returnable, imperious & melodramatic.
swim through on a modifier.
oddity's precursor.
announcers too spacey to continue...

new poem 1.8 |

red line. through. roughness fades the line.
imposes the line.
tunneling into where. is where.
where 'is within' sings george harrison.
improbable improbability. the lens leans through its dialectical promotions.
words are if defined. arē masked with identities
blotted paradises widely circulate a letterbox.
behold, beholding. so marginal entreaties.
lest oversight's endless game plan.

new poem 1.9 |

a precedent of ashcans.
praxis.
the tuner cleanses the keys.
priority over signature.
emeritus. debilitation's code-line is thrown windward.
commensurate infinity. let's measure the windward intelligence.
as a nominally too-verbal incandescence.
fragments behave it. dissent's too token so iffy amidst scrambling.
gone me pre-located.
india.
indexes.
we are willing throughout a marginalization.
we complicate trembling's ocean a define limn.
white or blanketed.
in the crease.
a threadless routine has its druthers before firing its throw-to—rope & snake.
doff.

stump.
nutshell.
throughfare identifications wholly decenter their no-fault assignment possibles.
adamant professors relate to the same precedents as begun though indifferent to indexical-hortense.
a mending wide strange & compound. straighten up. at last promissory.
amounts of this praise something awry.
the culinary stretch meets biases headless.

new poem 1.10 |

unit.
union.
unison.
yoda the magnificent.
distance & speculation.
i've seen a little star-wars.
gain & illusion of gain where sparks speak of minions to come.
teardrops unearth duple mainstays.
where it fits in is irregular.
nod when complexity hits, then define deletion & its martyrdom.
comparable the surprise settles in. keys loosen locks. i am bargained into closure but will dally here.
luge-noun fragments hold reminders of grunge.
the sloka is ungrammatical.
where stymied, retool.
there will be incalculable benelux.

new poem 1.11 |

a different moment. porcelain and chintz. solace if of the tiller.
no diadem whittles analogies met hale & hearty in surplus.
nitrates in foolscap try one's patience.
telephones topiaries & ocelots(oblique cats) in a dependent clause.
notions after the fact.
an itch so indelible it skanks crosswise around a corner.
in naivete is refuge as precedent calls itself a phoneme or actually three

phonemes.
a group of phonemes.
car tires on a sidewalk curbstone. whose retention reminds slowly?
topics-unroll-topiaries are parking lots away in the midland-midstream.
attentive to detection cover.

new poem 1.12 | [for carol]

incalculable entry dubbed & trusted.
let homeward, inner pliancy throw then as previously adapts.
melt mellow the cling harpoon, selected with attention.
extensions then so framed, the copier inverts letters midstream materializing.
ductile comparisons wear leggings of blue & gold so as to anachronistically throw to aligned melody.
each comparative bears heats show-cast on preview, so suits over box-lunch.
decoys without password gain no kingdom. summering flies are knowledgeable.
they took away the deposit.
mocha soundscapes clear for a ghostly paparazzo.
thoughts opt for realtime's oversight so forgone forlorn thematic to blend.
...to an attitude of dissent i retreat before resuming...
so sleepy the none-of-the-above holds its true disconnections as if promised but not so.
we choose parnassus without knowledge of consequence.
i broom a calliope that has had too many riders attached. i know that.
the friend of a friend receives something useful for attention & what chirps so awry prevails on winds on whom others can influence.
a real zone opens out if context does not abandon objectivity.
or illusoriness.
this poem claims there is no difference!
i am unknowable!

new poem 1.13 |

the tangible hotel indicates indicated reply.
a thorough & clearcut inlay of stone.
sonic discovery. bone in. bone there to behave beholding the karma beehive.
karma? i am an unqualified westerner. so it says on the platform of a shoe-soul.
the accretion of toil & effort is advised.

'inspiration is for amateurs' says a current pop-star*.
intractable ontology, or whatever.
some plaintive melancholic imbibers are comatose when they splay.
a definitive andiron scopes the holds on perpetual imposition through fallacy & mirage.
'it is acausal'. the motion speaks 'is'.
none of the above, each & every.

new poem 1.14 |

'nighttime the fable' is open.
retention's collocation.
once in an explosion the call is mended from attribute.
the least onset is thought to & for widening somatic empathy.
empathy's over-sought by some. crucibles are not always awaiting formulation.
in a tectonic shift, alternate visibilities team up.
the obsession wanders--hear it go forth!
rhythmic or not in its unbalanced ballast.
the forwarding march is non-statement.

new poem 1.15 |

'lotus, not confusion of actions', he said.
thought for the imprecation describes how das urteil is throughout the tale
modifying elongation
as the gist of a home-front so tangibly retyping oversell.
pitstop slowed for full cases--what substance it is?
to whom the knowledge is attributed?
while the dormant echelon as definition etches limitation forgoes tolerance is eager for topic: the throated vireo.

new poem 1.16 |

an apparition offline.
a cold aparition after factoring itself into itself.

manumission so it matriculates decently.
mindstyles have migrated over there before.
that is its praxis when flooded.
hold it a candle. switch it to reggae.
it is jocular into nighttime rising into cold sight.
to increase the heeding of plot-decoys.
thanks to evidences.

new poem 1.17 |

night.
redefine.
indelible.
chorus coexists with grabing.
milling with friends above & around.
colossal, the impunity of release that coils into a network-to-share.
immanent & capillary.
cappuccino.
a dove-tailed formalism is naturally parsimonious—
the waking cure.
a native orchestration of molecular betise.
combine. then allot.

new poem 1.18 |

a ghost in the canoe.
softened as w/ a public meteor.
agon for the close mentor's inductee.
non-sense is naive & expunged.—'i can't get me no.' *
detail's mode—scrupulous renditions form recollections.
it's decay willing a fissure—transit from one toggle otherwise othered.
a mode for abandonment none too often so majestic, minimally put.
so put the clock under a wall of clay.
one politic goes in to skulk while this goes.
c'est la vie...

new poem 1.19 |

history.
histrionic.
the cold emotional red-shift.
naive moebius that clarifies identity.
cold manages the thoroughfare on a silent omnibus.
where collarbones wrinkle an inner flange.
inner.
inwardness.
a descriptive term while operative or defunct.
dungeon signals dry out theatrical derivatives.
the cul de sac is admissive of too much entity.
it's a flange whose duple trends over the side.
noun-nuanced nuances call "illbient" the acrostic nature of wordmanship.
no harbor.
swordsmanship.
entourage.
the mannerist mannerism.
an ecological preoccupation that space remains.
a ludic habit entreated over rumors are yardarm.
so much disproportionate emulation thereof.
ghosts.
ayler.
verbal & visual.
without thinking we regulate.
the frequency debates itself.
so to engulf while capstans turn.
opiate-forming attitudes.
revert to sacks over holsters.
it keeps the peaceful dispensation.
it traverses targets ruled cleric mentor.
a tiger-balm for wounds given & received.
a contrasted motive relates cold spaces we inhabit.
a switch centralizes mandalas' connotation while the camera aperture impounds.
an etude wills to work wielding the very notions are thrown to impulse.
unfinishable.
yet idiom.
chockful.
we elope with a description that evolves.
description—the bias foregone of contention gone to a spelling bee.
some gustatory code—call it intrepid with a smile.

new poem 2.0 | for sheila

to description, then
the notions are parallel & obviated where bulleted.
emo grasping tells the frame to tap—no.
cul de sac.
they're livid through scuttling prescience≈.
a cartouche mollifies whodunits of a type opaque & glistening.
a mad materialism with grateful agreements.
they describe a presumed technique.
despondent motions are waiving looking at the lassitude where an emotion is spry.
how can colombes arrive as scepters?
so we mutate the items too pernicious to trash birdsongs.
indexed glances motivate topics.
throwness* is for once the artifact meeting with humanity.

NEW POEMS TWO

new poem 2.1 |

a ragged oval—
the thrown quorum runs on—
a deposit has oblique oblique ramifications—
those this, for example.
we catch frequent cellar wildernesses.
a gap is an inclusion.
dasein packs this not thereof that, then—
run on.
not earthsound—nor 'why' is uttered 'unknowable'.
the nimbus jettisons its behavior plugging 'fuzzbox' into google.
this culpable ontology runs through gear foibles
with leapfrog escargot impositions the rendition is soldered.

new poem 2.2 |

consequence.
trills.
a proboscis, thinkingly.
they run & fly.
why signal?
singing.
the yankees umbrella greeted with raspberries.
in some alternative reality.
test them, geodesic dome.
the crucifix details material geeks.
l'etape.
standard equipment.
some opinioned rind.
reminded of.
otherwise the irritating seeks the other.

new poem 2.3 |

'until' 'grammatizes' 'genealogy'.
it's an odd bookish emblem.
archeology with an attitude.
the wordy tenant crashcourses into agape.
reclaimed unity passes.
p.
o.
v.
threaded magneto.
blush—
footed blush threshes data.
the auditory embargoes the while.

new poem 2.4 |

a triadic kosa is in thrall with luminescence for-itself.
no bother for robust neurons.
cold speech.
the domain is foregrounded for music of behavior.
pleonastic therefores are recommend for their tact & grooming.
w are wanders no longer, perhaps.
thresholds crossed thirty-four years ago.
the gist of this poem's shortness is longterm.
these documents are overheard in house-shy borderlines.

new poem 2.5 |

the other contains fables.
recidivisms, blankets, meddlesomenesses, & delays.
incisive insight beholds trenchant mobs alternate with lions in the cellar.
mallets—diverticulitises—paradoxes—citizenries.
beleaguer them not.
happiness somewhat or contented is.
unroll bedding named for a trench.
at the graces of a canticle.

new poem 2.6 |

a modicum of familiarity.
soma behooves definition—
crawls that she blankets leitmotif.
quelled in self-defense.
the collider with a coiled palindrome.
so as to seek elementary particles.
we dream ocean.
we disrobe to swim.
pure.
confiding in speaking to a mirage over there.
an intention reflects on precedents milling about-face.
the nearby detail is no longer iffy or prosaic.

new poem 2.7 |

an interior flame.
willing so, the network is themselves.
free mainstays hold peccaries by the throat.
we wend our way.
negotiations 'midst other islanders.
no damage is done.
routines are soaked veritably.
baristas have meat-hooks on each finger so their innuendo is for effect.
arable, rinsed, & prearranged so a feature of thinking.
imbibe or reframe.
rhythms are welling forth ,
addendas are being broken.
why? — nonce.
where? — nonce.
when? — not.
there's more to iteration 'ere alignment sleeps.

new poem 2.8 |

under a tribunal a flange desists.
there's no tenet unless permission.
where is the claw? the hook?
this sophistic fantasy trills its literate cilia.
poetry invents a motif.
the motif is a jump from the ceiling
of itself.
is it correct to know how to invent.
discourse is a flourish.
quietude reacts to its momentum.

new poem 2.9 |

this melody is its own reward.
blue blushing bluntness blocks batting cages.
a pitcher.
a machine.

fertile diligence roves through each sentinel.
i am a person without double.
tapping on rattan makes aware of intolerable oversight.

new poem 2.10 |

the piano places itself on a plateau.
an utensil enthralls the quickness of hands.
now an embargo is prolated to infinity.
aspirates take sufficiency as itself.
noble citizens flare into their collective forests.
the impossible iteration is a lemming to the sky—
a precedent wills winnowing that waits for wanderers' total edification
toothed intelligently.

new poem 2.11 |

utterly composite where the ethical becomes necessity.
revering sorghum illbience in thrall of driveways--
public motions sport wily anomalies.
ingenuously predicated intolerables encapsulate when spotchecks are
disinfected.
errata rule.
control issues—
lack of.
sometimes an echt mensch is suggestive of conduction.
why the cranes fly by there.
go there.
somewhere someone speaks humorously about a clean breezeway nestling
sideways.
the bootcamp oversells might & gore.
naive is the sulk removed for wildness.
the space out is there interested meno mosso.
i am intentional & risking.
i carry forth authorial functions.
seek.
solve.
& remove.

new poem 2.12 |

3AM likes double-take are here.
rendered opaque for checking.
that resists or removes for bulk immersion.
imposition elector.
next...
incurably open the sky weans a demitasse.
refuel the elfin negotiations.
amnesia is all
darting from here to then.
quantified but not unqualified.

new poem 2.13 |

voices rile as the cone trolls a vidiot.
bobbed-created-visible.
toxic-salted-middle.
a tacked-rolling-mode.
the critter-consequences are great.
voices rile the conifer fortissimos.
['fortissimos' as a verb].
an impetuous mirage—
the tally proffers trumpets
for a centurion image
unadmissive of permission
opening a shuttered foyer.
friends cross the line.
off.
i restore it.
not.
it should not be there.
soma for a moniker bleached battiness.
no charlatan or igloo.

new poem 2.14 |

techno music as opaque as attitudes' meld.
the wan stunts recur sent throated into melodies.
sonnet what?
perhaps.
an additive miracle is a precedent at liberty for-itself.
sartre's radical freedom is in place—networked & coherent if one digs deep enough.
so imagines a materialization's plot while diamondine loops are held over a mineralized expanse.
tramps are set upon the critters listening rapt to the stillborn inside the head of a counterclockwise rotation.
the untold story nearby. without solace therefore.
motions on the horizon fraught with rhythmic description are not described.
no robber—no pawn—no sycophant—no entrance—all access.

NEW POEMS THREE
Autumn 2015

new poem 3.1 |

remain formal.
be aware of thoughtfuls of char-pits.
the tarn is wide.
a parallel memory is glossed over.
adamant to the endgame—hola & chokeberry.
whitely commencing & rarely so.
called an imperious teacher.
the ghat.
ghastly.
the occiput.
one hundred asleep counting. don'1 look.
no township.

new poem 3.2 |

he narrowly flees rare indices,
somatic rulerates are grieving.
the salute is behind intention,
briars waive consequences of a heroiade in a fore-begone room.
for what pretense are we gilding a gelding.
the comparison of charm compares with an intolerable decorum---
steep light parries its trustworthy phenomena.
call it attitude [sort of] pre-made & coerced.
blind indian wisemen seek the alphabet'd likening to kelp.

new poem 3.3 |

moot preciousness labeled might as one of its indelible chores.
aver the publicity notified with salute therein fortressed.
no walls against meddlers' burlap
how is the carnival silent for a moment?
the sequence is then and now from had been to promised.
the way out is nowhere.

new poem 3.4 |

hybridous talens are for payment.
here's the rent.
echo after echo, thoughtful emo,
while a bloss fulsome raiment adopts ghostly paradigms of truancy
the plodding materializes a numb clot over amounts of the phenomena's
double renderings holed up in an abnormal parking lot.
numerous defiances blot a retuning.
my manners pollute holdings bottled uptown—glowing preaching downtown.
there's a clutter everywhere listening to music hurled through the cosmos,
hoops and larks distort euphoric bluets knowing silence is not final—it is
closed through some appreciable motor-skills.
nothing else scavenged would fit the form when plus/minus labors are totaled.
the appliances are borrowed.
we are all borrowed.
so we harrow and yammer—

a pliable commencement leads to fiery blasts of liberation yielding silence
without emptiness!
the fulfillment is still to combine with intent.
hundreded over a climb of standards,
another attitude is balanced before hybrids begin to invent invasions of
bluntness.

new poem 3.5 |

i do not write of ennui anymore.
a state of mind is what experience holds in common with sideways steps over
the monday.
what is a monday?
a difficult song together-singing being rendered.
a wide-proof enduring salute & rhythm to theatre's orbit.
more the collaborations of innocences with a tattoo shop gracing no cluttered
lines on skin-defining solace as being here within space & time's rodeo.

new poem 3.6 |

oblique motion vanishes [blunted} from asterisk so brimful.
the tide of parry & flaunt begins this joist so oversold.
i announced an immense location so psychologically obssessed.
i am a bard of hypnogogic redaction.
this opaque methodology is hypothetical to tidy presentations.
hula hoops make sorties over the wall of silence defining addenda.
inner streets of the mind arrive confiscated without enforcement.
so on & on & further it goes—the compulsion startles what's held in face of
old symphonies.
theories doff crushed hats—bloss to their fabulosity.
who held mindstyles so wide so brimful?
who bartered with happenstance?
what was the case for innuendo so random?
hello is shampooed in oversight of denials.
so & so & so.

new poem 3.7 |

where contextualizing the middle—
then creeping through overstock that embarrasses vulcanizes attends the precedent flying far-reaching the distance blown awry.
politic answers are threefold-unrolling carpets.
omega deals alphabetics in wrappers,
even the amount is reluctant—
insomnia deploys hubris wherever hubris will go.
this is the part you'd call somewhat oceanic.
a rattan basement would hold more artifacts.
what is a collection of artifacts other than a sobriquet for eclectic dominos?
mundane thoroughfares behold nature as the demander implies selection before declension.

new poem 3.8 |

contra the role-playing karma,
there but for the gringo i are.
the role-player impends creature-comforts.
no one brings downtown helping cultural elements.
medicate the dwarf mandate.
what me in a mobius-like dwelling?
the beginning is clear,
we cannot know the endgame.

new poem 3.9 |

1] full blue moon in gloucester
confidential to the opal racetrack.

as moot as a smooth saloon
they degrammatize the defensive strain.

through release of tiathic envelopes
their dictum constructs blick-bling.

mandalas encourage intention to

consider & survive.
but where is obvious.
we are all there—
all here.

some various commentary of tools speak of what was
abstract phenomena,
recurring to speak of comma-variables.

detente contrary to evidence
the temporal/eternal concurrence of print.

in a briar often sketched we are sleepily
spotless to karma, tutenkamen's coil.

so cares the shoes of a vicar.

new poem 3.10 |

nine totals intellitext as immersion.
planet rime on the glass edge.
the millenary is bookishly debating with hopping frogs.
whose litigant is the chalk-white hand?
& just because having the motor-skills sometimes is not enough.
motive arrangements fall through attending cloud-covers behaving responsibly
wheeling a fermented logician.
call it sneeze to what you like.
a mountain of mouths to feed to treasures-in-hiding.
following though is the issue here.
new poem 3.11 |

knight takes rook's pawn, or some such other.
blue-green is in the room-surround.
on the outside or from the inside?
knowledge dawns slowly.
the heart muscle blushes.
lines change—roaming changes,
there is no wisdom to writing poetry.
the previous line is not true.
& even if it conveys opinion.
it is not mine.

new poem 3.12 |

children use the word "why" frequently.
and adults have to consider if it is an imposition.
perhaps it will alienate.
last night i slept three and a half hours.
who is the agent and the one receiving?
that it is mostly knowable is no mystery,
the big one is a longing for a personism.

new poem 3.13 |

the role of feral conduct iterates melancholy—
a rondelle-pitched bulletin wanders immerses collates.
dust-can poem, follow-ups are called in all senses 'feedback'.
give food back to the radiant heat-producers
some pages wear out their welcome mat going in the wrong direction.
the city empties out for summer-shine.
in so seeking a smartphone the world dumbs downtown by email-me beginning
their name.
imagine the world in a blog stored in an otter dam.
swimming forcefully on another occasion—
swimming the hundred-thousand islands' silent neutrality.

new poem 3.14 |

i am encircled with love—so says the mystic.
somewhere there is music.
i can send it anywhere i like.
perhaps or perhaps not.
that is not a logical conundrum—it is a choice.
my mind opens to unit-awareness.
contrasts define episodes' impetuousness.
someone arrives to the back porch.
the dog runs back and forth.
i don't know anything.

new poem 3.15 |

a swarm of pebbles writes elixir-behaving nothings.
liable to crash on bagatelles self-immersion while talking.
held tandem—the replica can be modest.
it opines 'meow' gracefully.
pleonastic home-front.
gapped nightshade where defensible.
moods implode hourly--then scamper.
awaits if a gated city, notions while demanding notions.
believers nettle amazement hundred times overload.
weeds in the front garden are not singular--we distribute any ilk removable.
it was once another ideation waited for indication and was not.
a total awareness of sound through sense-defined manners.
geeks wear tee-shirts dyed black & orange with inked cloth.
halloween wakes to attendance its threefold attitudes network on holidays also.
i sit in the same place, joining yearlong rapidity, with pelicans and seagulls.

new poem 3.16 |

held-in-transit tuesday—
walked through awash in an nth of paradigms.
the notion wah-wah-oeuvre plasticene-metal-and-cuckoo.
how does a threshing stampede establish fondnesses.
there fools gympish & holy ascribe work to rationality.
vocation imitates relationships—or iffiness is backwards.
intrepid agora—world & signal neutrality pushes a wheelchair where 'when'
begins its receipt for data.
begins wiring domes for hubris.
gardez-toi.
the ruddered ship has no motor-skills emanating ourselves into the air.
a month of precedent reveals snowfall on the jnanin's episode.
'l'estranger' clocks days & months—
renascent rumors alter waiting.
replacement mirrors hold onto an advice wiring haptic veils.
why not derive a forgiveness beholden to attentive precedent.

new poem 3.17 |

cortez & why whytofore comes to mind.
in barter this wave awaiting another. contrastive amulet.
late bloomer.
dossier thereintofore for waiting milliseconds later.
agonist on guitar, that killer of guitar skiffle.
aptitude singing soaring motiveless except to scoff at multiform plebians.
duffers, all, emulating voices from improbability
voices from removed arrangements.
we walk downstairs then outside to a chair to write.
three and one make four, but why?
has it always been like that?
even before the universe?
this is a presentation from mac text-edit
on a porch from this road.
it is impulsion to continue that capitulates
& blots out camaraderie,
an island of dog-barks interrupts the buzz of crickets.
waiting on the moment, so meanders the less than one.
more than ten billion.
out here on this screened porch the mosquitos keep their distance
knowing full well to be here is to be on an island highway.
disturb nothing, do not disturb.

new poem 3.18 |

trains.
goers.
a stymie from and to.
try to read a schedule of ministrations from potency.
who defends amounts of presence there opening?
a syntax-summit releases persistence dominating leonine clashes.
rams lock horns on a frozen tundra.
holding steady—the fable of affect is thought to be else & more perfect.
it is not.
some frantic melody zipped the mouth of mindstyle.
descriptive announcements have beads on the neck of a woman.
yon befuddlement is rated geologic moodswing.
senses reverie sturm und drang hold more & more.
when simpatico, thresholds, portals, dramatic pauses—

ixnay on a address not visible from the road.
is a rostrum or what it is.
no answer is forthcoming—i don't like the role placed over me.
actually many roles, so many situations, there contrasting hand held in
emulating previous accuracies.

new poem 3.19 |

seeing irony glow frankly opens meddlesomeness.
a concern for bulletins mitigates the context applied.
elemental, dear mall-a-be-free.
so green the forest immerses clothes-horses where they may.
'sheep may safely...', wrote j s bach.
a lozenge waits ornately for the mouth that feeds it.
hola!—i was a mirror wherever i wished to be,
rain, torrential rain—
where did you grow to in the underbrush?
so, who are you to talk & write like this—
even having a computer speak your lines?
or else i walk away natural & sheepish—
wounded before a cloud can catch fire.

new poem 3.20 |

until the mosquitos become moonlight,
how transited the flare offering a soapbox million to you,
is the notion without broaching of difficulty.
mindstylism everywhere.
people the flame ofand portal to the ministrations of glissandi.
so epilogues decant amulets one by one over the capitals of big countries.
extremism agrees to redefine treaded mirages' meaning.
a legume grows in brooklyn nearly every day.
previously, thousands of waking sounds were remitted in person.
four hundred people in the audience tonight.
thank you for being here.

NEW POEMS FOUR

new poem 4.1 |

how much is the doggie in the windows.?
otherwise composite and totally unknowable.
memory of a toad.
happiness is a keen immersion in the totality of the universe.
human posing complicates everything.
the time of day is not the same as the motion of the stars
the stars change their patterns minutely & continually with no apparent rhyme
or reason.
we are not a in stasis.
everyone renews all the cells in their body every seven years, i've heard.
what is rhyme?
what is reason?
tools to be used sparingly.
somewhere someone sometime is the rule.

new poem 4.2 |

combining attention-spans is not like disapproval or reticence.
while ignoring truth-after-truth does one arrival mean as much as the other?
please act courteous.
do not wear a 'fear no fear' tee-shirt—
it will advertise your youth as literal.
mending shins is a subroutine of deserved parries—
not from this camp, though.
let me write, let me paint—
then i'll know the world is d=l=r=o=w and more than s=d=r=o=w.
my computer can write vertically—
or so it claims
someday i'll give it a l=r=i=h=w.

new poem 4.3 |

a rogue infinity crawls over the icy streets.
the spiel is that 'poetry' is different than 'text'—
and between those is 'writing'.
what distinguishes them from each other?
'poetry' is aesthetic, read out loud at 'poetry readings'—
i try not to go to poetry readings.
'texts' are more experimental in nature
having the aura of sanctity over them—
at least. so it's said.
for instance, religious 'texts'.
i do 'writing'—trying to be free as possible in the form of 'poetry'.
'writing' can be anything—
even have no outward distinctions.
categories mean nothing, it could be said—
they are merely a convenience.

new poem 4.4 |

thursday. late night.
the clocks are on backwards.
not only do ateliers walk backwards
but chandeliers will need one hundred different synonyms.
the chandeliers' synapses detail a regimen of no gluten, no sugar,
and less salt. fundamental changes arrive around handmaidens of purity-itself—
while the symmetry of increase and decrease is the same.
cycles are like circles that run with the tides.
seagulls screech in gloucester
so a mindstyle is preserved.

new poem 4.5 |

a wanderer supplied fiction from where 'when is now'.
replicated pop-survivor minus-plus pop=pop-pop.
trolling phrenologists discern the wiles of a gullible audience.
metals form holograms where silence once was.
'nature always unwinds' i've heard it said.

nevertheless, a blind prophecy derides no one.
omissions commissons—
covered by language

new poem 4.6 |

where i sign signal nieuw agenda genuflect & parry those fortitude beholds.
denizens—wary operatives culling motor motions kicking hidden in rumorese.
those fabulosities remind feint cackle thorough dispolitic that memory;.
olde that the cringe nefertiti gnashes calamine loofa spoons—deterrents.
imagining elemental elementation then thensone retinol chances changes.

new poem 4.7 |

modalities—'after you gaston'.
ad hominem for telephone synergy.
the opening chance channels oddity.
when there is nor pyre nor crosswise—
the optimum iteration goes fallow.
morning birds make scolding sounds as i sit here to write.
a presence operating modes through song & chant.
somewhere an angel pours milk for the capillaries of the king
who entrances himself with poised charms.

new poem 4.8 |

a combination of immersion & technology
recalls of omission.
text-radar blown away to the happenstance
not harassing global clime.
tale of the preoccupation.
retain pliability while sliding through
upbeats,
the remission of 5-part-songs is while watching
an old teevee.

crashing clouds through intramural contrasts
tactful or not, the mahogany salute resembles
a cruet where politic mannerisms vanish before
legumes flourish.

new poem 4.9 | [unfinished poem in 5/4]

a colar exchange of collars would wake good choice.
the birds outside are scolding as i write this.
there's rain to delay the game that wanders through a day of literal majesty.
bless the harvest.
bless this choice, aware of while the roaring sands grate through what doorway is the flame.
someone outward to me invites/volunteers the many others however their existence.
moot tenancy blossoms while drywall is constructed.
the only chance this coheres is kneeling before a moodswing.
go to change the routine.

new poem 4.10 | [unfinished poem in 3/16ths]

major d'omo calling the kettle blank.
for no reason.
while opening or a scarfing down of pizza or some such other.
the kettle's blackness is without control.
thereto opening a concern—
leaving tangible misconstrual...

new poem 4.11 | ['woe is me' poem]

it's an opaque mirror on the wall.
sighing.
a root canal, a bridge, one extraction and two caps.
aunt winnie'd groan a large 'oh vey',
as wooden chromatic scales practiced by students everywhere

descend & ascend, descend & ascend.
raining where somethings don't go for a long time
and others are chosen straight away.
everything has a preparation time & space.
mr einstein taught me that.
once in a wave of light i caught a foible called 'the arts'.
fantasy football is far away from housing the rules of the game i play.
somewhere intractable motions claim what's left of definitive mannerisms.
etched on a graffiti acknowledgement of change is nothing else after the fact of intentional homage.
so, i collect what's left of the open chairs &
bear brunt of which aperitif grandstands out-ranger preoccupations.

new poem 4.12 |

please do not complicate what is simpler than
dropping a coin onto a charm.
it's already there—
that which in affect becomes additive.
cold cutlery arranged in rows & columns—
& why?
[...motor skills of a moron collect atrophization
when rolling to barter with slaves...]
'can you hear me knocking?' sings an old pop song.
we are already waiting.
do entertain any notion voluntarily—
as the crosswise dauphin reflects while engaging chicken-proof-wired contractors
to phrase a contemporary additive on what's international & paisley.
not impressed—
are words collecting ashes in the corridor.
we are too early to lift baggage.
no one washes midstream anymore, it being too dangerously appetizing.
this has been called 'a stray mind'—
get used to it!.

new poem 4.13 |

it's an opaque mindfulness, 'illbience'.
...nine-letter word i coined.
always.
is healthy.
a condition of...
then.
as when in motion the accrual of decorum.
as however a parroting written above & about.
unlikely the torsion of callousness looking at what's nearby.
so wide the concept. so malleable it is.
as when flying through a fogged sky tuned to nothing special.
why while attending to absence does an intuition of exactness flow from
fingers used to practicing classical piano.
...that which i no longer do.
a contract elsewhere has been happily signed.
cool idiomatic sanpaku person i are not.
shelving that line the opaque homage is stepped up.
...mannerisms in the midst of a crowd.
'a stray mind' and why not? it is.
choices everywhere where why? is not answered.

new poem 4.14 |

as at the border of infinity & zero
whenever that error occurs
no acknowledgement reverts
to rehearsal 'one more time'
nor agape at the larger increment ahead.
small precious meandering solace & stray mind
that folds where mindfulness holds opacity
each lettered motion vanishing as sands
while decanting voice or signal,
symbol or meaning, thereof to decide
a citation a colophon assuming politic
narration evaluates telephone conversations
is it who oversees a natural decoy—
loitering in retreat, snail-paced.
big yeller nearby, the contrast is intact.
lunch hour goes by in this busy restaurant

defending the word lighted on this screen.
some long-faced operative closes down this
shout-filled room. not at fault, the laughter
is aware of happy children nearby. so much
confetti, these words, someday i'll write a
'real' poem.

new poem 4.15 |

a land's blocker, voicive & perfunctory,
combining various jalapeno specialisms.
tunneled into parallax—
affect grips the world
& is winnowed from friday into saturday.
& complicating this from before hearing this—
& there's a notion nothing changes in repetition.
incorrect or correct doesn't matter
& whether we tell is also without point.
let's wait it out.
some comparative unreality is most likely why—
with time an indeterminate psychology
would be held responsible for sharing that
plasma's physiology is without map.
shoring up the prenuptial is impossible—
better meld a borograve.
an addenda within the same century—
name from frequency held in mind—
tassels hold pardons for their sleepy renegades—
a compressed world is intent on
sparing wildernesses embracing years or millennia.
share one pod—
repeat ornaments—
oversold & underpaid.
in fact,
overworked, understaffed &
underpaid is the theme
whether sung or pebbled.
let's define me—
simple or complicated—
a token perfection that never materializes.
hoodoo economics has been replaced with

hoodoo ecology—
i don't know what is worse.
my thought is: it will take a lot longer to get
used to the effect of hoodoo ecology.
someone outside is speaking with a mega-
phone.
just then a tin can is thrown through
the open summer window.
i think i'll put on some headphones and listen
to some music.

new poem 4.16 | [in lee, ma]

while the walk light blink-blink-blinked assigning value go emotion—
some valley protrudes motionless caveat blossoming
where the glow ahead
some motor-skills vanish dallying in chasms.
blunt from levitating to a response volitionally public not imagined
a corporeal motivation elicits shards waited for in sloth or in that emotion.
i thought to myself,
'hold still & keep breathing—
just keep breathing'.
emotion of air through the windpipe seemed visibly one-headed.
there would be no discussion period apres ski.
a commonality of purposive amity resides well into the evening
as the new car starts
into drone actuality with not a sound to awake
which was surprising.
...still breathing—
...checking for that body-response—
a greeting was before the clock ran down-street with a broom.
many strangenesses combine the rules of syntax
taken for comedic invisibilities—
solved in context for narrowly-fed authority—
each the influence is bagged, ingested and ferreted liminal.
constraint jumps the gun of sere-incalculable resists
what hand holds the hand that holds the hand
of mystery
if one looks an endgame straight in the face
it is life itself that keeps on living.
what else can be revealed in spacetime

is consulted in solitaire.
the whole wide world is sonatas for brunch—
& blankness where silence ought to be.
'plink down yo' nickels & dimes—tens & twenties—
who tells in what epoch alchemy began?
somewhere over the rain-bell no doubt'.
that's what leaning-on can do for/to an entity,
there on the rocks waiting to be zapped.

new poem 4.17 |

the levitation of abandonment
flies the midnight route northward.
without claimants, a varying ocean defers to
anyone having atari or floating on a clarinet.
people who warm erase coral reefs
woolens are sought outside the home
once a day only the viceroy seeks politics
and that at the exercise room.
the most interesting man does not read a
newspaper, he gets news from the internet.
less and less and less and less no matter
how you cut it up an arrangement of sound
recalls itself one day at a time playing such
cliches purring through a crowded house.
mindstyle adapted from tenners on unthink-
able boats walled into photocopies harbors.
ennui is old school. permission is not granted.
it is not allowed. this keyboard is loose.
there's a zine about loose canines. why be
loose when sham burins hold attraction for
a larger percentage of the population. i've
always been a crowd pleaser. see me on the
music stage, full of found opinions, promul-
gating the errata of winding lakes onto into
out of that is activity for activity's sake is
worth considering, that is, 'not'. a halo around
the surface of the mountain checks the run-on
sentence or the run-down stronghold, without
a thought foregrounding the attribution found
elsewhere nowhere faster than that then soon.

new poem 4.18 |

no tarrying in the cloud fields.
rules mount cold & sinkhole connoting a mimosa or a florin.
as the notion of where influence is ironic—& from.
melding heroic as the edge of an updrafted-word on a cliff.
i caught trance nation on teevee without a shear cliff to behold.
unfurling a flecked-beetle heals a hand of shorn intent.
earthling, wait in the window across the street
as the minou becomes sniffling-reeled—
someday i'll understand from where the fire-fountain
was lit.
glitterati pounce on the farm-fountain of spades & clubs.
the women grapple with their queens & diamonds.
the entrancement of charm reflects on them as
one solid chunk of sheet rock that is different &
cannot refuse its thought
as it is.

NEW POEMS FIVE

new poem 5.1 | [dialogue]

waking.   the concept railing from & to.
shard.   nothing held over a flame.
fold.   loose canyon. the combination.
re-tone turn.   grimace to drumbeat. offand.
those nation icons.   contravene billy-clubs.
multiplexer.   addenda to luxury stereophonics,
                                blood blotted by porcelain.
far=away.   eyes in the back of my headrest.
the theatrical.   image of personism glowing.
the immanent   we are immersed in intention.
mocha.   contravene for surreal mindstyles.
tornado.   or tsunami. no thanking yours.
bulletin.   abbreviated.

concertino. concertina locus the flamboyant.
valiant motive. whether to do nor no or not to do.
wanders. mind minus content meandering means
wanes widely. just who you run with across the pike.

new poem 5.2 |

it is commotion that imposes items enthralled without blunder.
hello helio, what's your matrix flaunting today?
some ambulatory creature livid civilian bleats moodswing from candle to chandelier.
nothing would please more meteors balancing through therefores and absolutisms.
a small poem would suffice—however it's the long-form extricates us.
federal questions admitted once on a shelf—
the impulsion for/from while standing still holds heliotropes.
fortunate for youtube's free music-listening service.
patterning columns introspections midstream in life's journal.
sweeping the porch stairs again & again & again—
zen exercise when your master orders it.
amacord waited for wonderfully kaleidoscopic introductions.
hoping through the night—shelving through the night.
vehicles downtown running lights to get there in an unnecessary hurry.
slow down the engines—shut down the engraving plates.
small-time big-town—the execration of mercy.
while contrasting the smoothest imports smothered yet.
harrowing threefold impetuosity greets geeks silently perishing—hola!
youtube remembers my previous selections in choosing songs to recommend to me.
arrangements reopen anxious matters forming while transitory agendas remain overhauled when comparisons flunk.
bylines blur the geometry of a rainstorm holding out for a chance throughout the night.
other-waves signal persistence opaquely motionless in cahoots before justice—
that's the swirl of irony shelving a flash-drive before savory complications drift away.
a cricket pours its hearing freely then returns for a giraffe a concept a memoranda an earful an imposing a motion—
while from before there's nearness 'neath an apple tree.
the setting sun on the green-greedy lawn forms patterns of small bits of light thrilling to see.

healing the either/or dichotomy has been the challenge of many philosophers.
the choice to contrast that imposition genetically is where to blend the two is complicated or simple—
which you choose is very important...
the surface hastens before abysses are jump-through-thereof-therein overcome.
holding one's own oeuvre transigent—an ethos ditt- ditto-ditto before saying 'goodness gracious—'.
typing the reminder of dreamtime one shelf away—one book on that shelf.
a so-much-needed part two imitates together-tigers from the get-go.
everyone's theatre-gems took ethics one step further.
tantalus without the frippery.
homeroom geraniums blossom before the frost becomes apparent.
hoops & we've been shown the before & after while demanding adaptation.
reveries of cherry-cola—weekly introspection before a greeter.
please form no lines—muffle no gasps—return from webs

new poem 5.3 |

motion-cahier thisness so voluntary it embraces loka-wide precious words.
indelible watermarks over a silence so largo that it behaves well to be elsewhere.
immersing, negotiated in a melancholy
thereto so politic that transfers are theatrical entities due their suchness.
it is one sheer ascent to thrown impossibility that no erroneous ceremony contains the bluster-thrall of picket fences.
well-knit & careful as a cartoon shown to hearing thought of a voluntary insertion.
no talk.
jabberwocky islands are here to pave—
the etiology if the world-whirl touches a rehearsal of motives
all it is grappling with is arrays holding others' terms.
we fleece the genome by reifying somatic virtue—
shards are—
else the yelling story stopgap
|on the table with ether coursing its veins.
it's a small mystery the distanced magnets—
revoiced motor-cast thresholds of music—
thresholds beholden to calisthenics of discourse no longer as.
vivaciously free!

new poem 5.4 |

whose pride renames the fuel-can operating system?
so sullen the moped get-goes behaving well before intimacy.
the demonstration of affect is nearly lost when sleep takes over—
but the sacred orbit of that reminder is not welcome.
hola—the permission sought is not forthcoming.
winning is narrowly over-rated.
i think it's mr dylan has a nice line i'd quote if i recalled correctly.
a law of precision is the iteration needed here.
the organism behaves inside a warren to battle itself out to the oceanside.
a watershed of emotions that will never have other ways is too boring.
change is a notion unreal to those people not aware of that they could be aware
of what they are not aware of yet.
as a semantic inventory this natural impression is strong & intractable.
so why not & why not?

new poem 5.5 |

onto role-platelet thematics.
we are a guardian of emptor-melancholy.
crowds of latency—
clouds of description so indelibly enraged.
so multiple is the form the attitude is thereof a vast heresy—
a decoy by abiding in relata—
errata of the mesh cordillera.
addressable that unrolls in duettino—
some other altruistic voice—
the next fealty more than excision.
so predictable thorough knit as a tie bo-ho boo-hoo.
echt gehesmene desk-jotterthink of ibm curio.
snack food junga-loo—
tarzan & jane play at abstraction.

new poem 5.6 |

when style opaques selfhood,
there's infinite trouble. throughfare to
unfinished unreasonability, not longer
malleable to cornea. implicated in
mnemosyne is gravity and rearrangement,
somewhere bolstered implacable for
a mod-ten-twelve impartition.
while echoes guard creation, spiritual
eminences hold
which candle chance balances out
the books of forward emotion.
in looking for you, an ocean of
sighs in this implausibility
coiling this way & that.
a box of clear-breaking cereal—
the faster the breaking.
comparing which element thought
endures is naturally opaque
there is loiterers outside
our window, we hold evidence
against them unfairly—
perhaps the dog's new bone
is not a change-of-subject-cube
for her. her agenda is always
wise.

new poem 5.7 |

ecstasy reveals itself in a revel together with a button-knotted cobra tamer.
the words speed away once wondering then softly previous.
a party at their house is not the normality of aftereffect.
the pitch of the roof is also a quantifiable effectuality narrow as a short-gauge-railroad.
10 smiling cartouches blast through the window with out a briton's classes.
haggard-eyed thoroughbreds elect themselves or someone of that-there ilk.

new poem 5.8 |

i am interested. interested in the possibilities inherent...
where not unpolitic & there suddenly appoints amphitheaters solid in your camp.
an inconsequential unconsciousness blots impressions out of card-members' numeric coasts.
one two three four—now five—where else the foal-gentle-oaf somatic to reboot.
mindstyles running everyone wherewith holding eminence where plausibility enrolls.
intrepidity emulates on-time schematics—& why not?
blunt emplotments arrive where solemnity introduces petalisms north of silence.
the silence orpheus demands is parallel to interpretation.
somewhere someone defines no hat-check before entity.

new poem 5.9 |

intractable emotion.
logged ingestion of rivulets porous stake-shot bureaucracy
once telling self-seldom hurrying over the candled self-smitten
lobbed into room's center.
bylines imply overhead egoic lariats on either lighthouses or black-light.
satisfaction's myopic leniency unfurls reified scalar hinges—
is that on mending quaffed inquiry?
it's a shock gentility cannot abstract from defensive anomalies do not prepare
for the walk-light to change to green
before the curfew holds further steady.
bias controls orchestrate block-grants-
mapping solace on walls of sleet-sheet-sleet rock walls of ice & grime—
thoughts are held in the background-operating engagement
railroads of permissiveness en route torrents mill thresholds silently.
behavior called grassroots weave donor-profiles in & out of memory.
precision instructions often err—
attend to when it becomes one towards that—
we imply edicts—remove edits bleed what is normality's site.
advancing mirrors call out for feasible storied sites
smoked & snorkeled within the neighborhoods.
a grasp into relata [called 'memory' or other in other cases] proclaiming.

new poems 5.10 |

where vouchsafed thresholds implicate denials—
onsets of dimming the light are precedents not yet fully in cadre with motionlessness.
once beheld in can-do witnessing motions exult noteworthy that signal overshot & prevailed.
oily food genetically pure , very free—
oil of the tobacco likely implacable & making its memoranda one step over the line
so we stand our ground,—having been there so long.
a recall of which partaking is empty or full
please to surround millings where silence is reversed.
the reversal of silence is more the cameo of itself to shred ears with its loud voice.
while imbibing that spirit of education, as long as the recorded beget their own modes.
it is its own moods tracking the rehearsal from one space to another.
a summation of versatility where one is where one goes to its other point the other side of the sky—
which was here first?
the enjoyer is none other than me—
please try to disprove it!
a hold on one's answer is best.
there's no one shelf dominates the world of words.
the word-world is at best a patchwork quill of reeff-tanglels.
perhaps as the solace of myopia is to not equal treading over snow-tracks.
animals in the winter woods—in the autumn it's the autumn woods.
one intelligence detangles the other,—a motivea at time.
so protean the resistance, once pertinence holds itself over a candle—
there's no telling where a chaise lounge or a teardrop on the face of the person on that fancy chair will pop up.
i am a silent witness—i report this to you—-
you determine to replace your coat on your lap
while sitting there on the chair, so valuable, you paid so little for,

new poem 5.11 |

where the ocean upturns its stolen attitudes
bloodhounded intelligent tomorrow's quotidien.
weal of propriety—
who hastens praxis in the of face of wrung hands.
shell of turtle, shell to tyrant—
why else difference?
what similarity?
from a small cocoon i turned—
small plastic jewels opened—
they were really flowers.
the large of the three waited table tiers on one's shoulder—
ready for a long-time weal of grommets.
one is stasis held in abeyance—
to the emotion combining context & essence without bloat—
one served the other—
those persist drifters.
salesmens' offers blink opaquely in the harsh light.
rankled chair, thoroughly demolished by its lack of content,
but the per-audient needn't know of that.
how can that be a contraction of that?

new poem 5.12 |

nature torrero. knit robust gneiss-laden rafine walled with shist.
melodies swarm around a motive for remoteness—so unfortunate.
going north those repay ingestion's holding martyrdom somewhere else—
isn't that the frequency—jimbo?
met with on a holiday in venice—
not a holy day for certain.
entrapment from the more of the same inching to obliquity.
waking to grasp the geranium held in front of holding's motion.
mouse-catcher—wide of signal—not outside in nature's solar description.
sunset heals lasts longer the tone light waiting to change anywhere.
simple those persist—because it's a poem & it must be said.
waking to hearthful notions the reopened hearing heart negotiates with
selfhood's center—a rarity nestled on the encroachment once shorn of praxis
those oceans well-knotted at head's top.
a tilde for your purpose—so a siren is not more begone that roles can play at
rules while waiting for lightness of heart to enter.

new poem 5.13 |

detail.
pursue the bready river.
there's no cadre with widening otherwaves.
alfredo, what would we do w/out each other's orbit?
mead of the syllogism, beware.
hold to enigmatic restatement whenever dry—
contrary & vigilant.
reset button.—
bob dylan.—
planet waves.—
i'm totally lost.—
bordered in on the camaraderie, there's no exit—.
there's someone to ask whose information is everywhere—.
blustering where big-shots hold butane lighters.—
emptily oceanic.
i am increasingly more & less plausible of the chimney soles—.
licorice is no washer overcome in oleander.
absence is a hoot.
baristas crawl over the kingfisher.
the kingfisher dislikes coffee.
notions crash around state-house buildings then restore to new hard drives.
wending our way to a gypsy eddy.
naturally einsam was along.
another indication behaved well-before the candles were snuffed outside
thereof—
swimming through whose ice-house no one could enter.
shelves of meat & cheese lined the walls.
a poem ornamented every wish.
reactions needed no response.
treble & bass clefs meant the same notes.
there was no making-unequal.
musicians became confused.
not so once it all became apparent.

new poem 5.14 |

contrasts the coeli then it is solemn.
midi those the costa del sol
contact with.

meteorological etymologies span the universal—
the astrophilic music is platelets.
a smartest world implies detail & expansion—
delicacy & remoteness.
aleatoric nuances are tobogganing where
while some ask questions.
a super slowdown—ironic that some iterations behave
believe where others are going southward.
zones of purity—zones where that is no question.
how comparison-ing defend delay & proceed partake—
we'll never divulge.
neil young's cover band is on the box—
raid the glow says cortez.
he is not playing that guitar.
is the expulsion final?
no voice is satiated yet.
no voice will tell of it.
the world will continue with parallax
sweeping up the cinders.

NEW POEMS SIX

new poem 6.1 |

there has opened a nowhere calling itself imminence.
details forthcoming.
read above it—
salt is motionless & pliable worn thin from solvent so brine—
called oversoul by some.
a captive ocean intends tiered-gardens—motivate by sentient-power.
'when the power of love, overcomes the love of power—there'll be peace.—jimi hendrix
well, he said it not me—
though i might have forty-five years ago, had i that awareness.
so many passages—so much time—so much the looking forward & backward
—
& a new perspective somewhere else.

new poem 6.2 |

milling about therein
fortitude congeals into
melees of dogs &
picnic benches.
we ache at the dog park.
dogs don’t know what to do
but they do it next.
that which they don't know what to do.
comparable to intention is inclination—
one is more concerned to force—the other
a vote to remanded comprehension
one step ahead of the other
while others sleep the matinee through
a gesture not thought out previously.
gasp!

new poem 6.3 |

the mountain is a composite picture.
sitting opposite—nature naive concerning...
while connotating elegance opulence mirror-driven salutory.
look up those adjectives—bilge & salvatiion empirically dour.
while ghosting emcees a renamed motion partakes spotted partisans—
the rendition deepens where solidarity is the clue, bottomless is a rented house.
so many preclusions devote lifetimes in cathartic losses.
the downstairs flair is wary of a culmination chanted on parallel scales of the octave.
please replace my conjurer’s implosion—outer turned inner.
what is ‘outward’? what is ‘inward’?
a wise friend years ago said ‘there is no ‘outward’’.
i took to mean ‘it’s all ‘inward’’.
with a lot of consideration i have in all honesty—
no reason to doubt that original ‘inner’ voice.

new poem 6.4 |

sailing into the sycamore-sky we fall where there is no punishment.
a blank string of words were the greeted mindstyle overhauling attention.
songstylism woke before planetary nuance—of this i am sure.
listening was before reading.
& threefold habitats endured well into their ninetieth years.
plastic wheels on feet of style—the ornamental dossier washed from habit—
why combine where scansion & containment was enough.
so relative & approving—the guitar practically wrote its own song.
pleasing gestural breezes—contracted asterisks one after the other—
the matinee washed over by cornichon— genetic change alternatively change
alternatively disabused and rehearsed.
so let's get involved in a bubble-rubbing contests.
how ribbons retain contacts retainues without accessing conscious arrays
iterated outside the rewarded classic ocean of sighs.
employed mid-stream in songs of human warmth—or was it songs of humanity.
such an abstr act word: humanity—.

new poem 6.5 |

realms of existence probed—noted as mainspring.
where pliant the commotion seems to be cloning itself.
for existence's glyph--the impetuous thought is melting away--
an affect that explicates itself well.
remove behavior as deified & motionless.
on with cross-legged meditation smiles.
let's visit this complex once in a while.
not impossible for lettered amalgams to vanish...
the spotted intention holds solidarity with pursued missives.
telling the sophist of mirages held before one's eyes is not the answer.
this emotion is wide & discursive.
ifs khakis blot out silent houses over the fence somewhere core silence.

new poem 6.6 |

we are what we are, no apologies==what you see is the economy of desperation
—no wait perspiration and desperation. some alternation phlegmatic eye-sore-

blooms so it rejoins cogently the siren noted to exceed on parallel parallel action. the strange right-of-way, a club med materialism dramatic moods so battery-driven dwarfs vexing the soft touch long-term values. plastic envelopes exemplary incursion that motions fenestrated by innocence at the star. so, we want to know 'y'al' about-face on the beach shell generalities driven through person

new poem 6.7 |

less the emotion,
gain a colisseum-solidarity.
plus that other's grievance breaks down imperious. dawdle amidst yoga sortleges, this totem toned schismatic voluntary topple-tottering where scry. that ipseity of melange touting acumen over their head-streams. blue chakra voices weal trepanning solidarity toiling tandem that illbient minority. at least overhauling balance-systems efficates delirium grouped as cell-wide. the solemn portent waking weevils denied salutary basket-weaving.
a fortune oeuf-literal middle-streaming a cluster of noun to verb shifts, become-visible become-invisible snappy-cold literati oversought in meep-as-minus delays. announcing the delay of handsprings—the visibility of candelabras & closures—impassive where solved icons blur details.

new poem 6.8 |

is there a difference between an illusion & an illusion.
emotons replace nothing else—that's their strength.
cadmium red medium glows like no other—
too bad it's extra poisonous.
big smiles have turned into hard knitting.
eloquence bottles itself into body-after-body—
the flow is to imbibe & decapitate itself
and well before knowing—
it solves itself.
an example:
one time a crowd walked along an ocean inches before
whose emptiness walked one trillionth of a second
heedless offering plotted cosmic.
then that watered-down ocean immerses a locus between flavors the harmony

of blind inversions.
the kangaroo-possibilities' warmup of ten-thousand leaves it there on the wall to be read.
as a shift in tone it was immersed some new genome.
a blurry invention delayed by nothing paradoxical.
whose complexity wove
which prelude was/is battled outside worries genies
engulfed therein descend to survey pretense & regurgitation.
not a roadblock—
inroad the telling named pell-mell which serve genuinely the adaptable
restrictions behaving as doldrum are dissolved.

new poem 6.9 |

gliding through infinity, what combination etches descriptions of beheld impass.
mettle of the absolute rhythm so seasonal in challenge, challenged, trusting.
shards begin the remoteness liberty ensconces where plied, oblique.
motion integrally open & opener—nowhere open & shut—
rebuttal of emptiness—cadre of lotus warriors—
loiter no longer—the whirling implicates who stands still—
so it says the returnable —that to motive named license—
is poetic, even.
music is its own recursion—the scholar doesn't know why.
hidden intelligence opens when eyes do this literality.
feckless the engarlanded poseur knows only method—
while potency imbibes finesses—one solved proclamation—
entente lottery—gavel in coeli—difficulty is imagined.
wrap heedlessly around the material of the world.

new poem 6.10 |

moon rocks in hearing range. shouting range. over there, in fact, inference from detail only.
choruses in arranged contingency—.part of a studio—students everywhere—
who is theorem-defending, who not?
are i to which the compared rollerskates in development?
wildernesses of terraces beleaguered by imagination only. not untidy or sparse

—

the portions not deleted are mostly practical—
you are believing mirrors' bagatelles by beethoven—bach wrote no bagatelles—
i played no bagatelles except possibly schubert's—if he wrote any—& if i played them—.
the classical music days are adjourned—judgments amidst definition calling themselves law is different than music's muse ontologically present.
huddling the twined overlord implies nothing but secular exegesis.
whose partaking of irony calls time's passage the mobility offered & desired.
ternary notions crop up in the shallows of complacency.
too-strong portions snicker the haphazard—
those repaying untold definitions.
a definition was seen yesterday walking toward ocean road—
the way was steeplechased amidst rare earth metals—
contrasting in the contradictions bottled before apperception of anyone living was aware of itself.
someone offered me a beer, i chose water—make mine 'spring'.
'spring water' is the water drunk all year by poets conscious of time's non-passage.
us others live on from before and beyond seasons are counted.

new poem 6.11 |

contesting thought's introspection—
a grammatical nature voices one's cage of mannequins
on white backs around & repulses the featureless.
'i asked for water, she gave me gasoline,' sings howlin' wolf—
gasoline—i drink ice coffee by choice.
child of the cafes i are, companion to monsieur baudelaire.
where surcease into emotion's layers & delays arrive
in safe harbor.
we are fringed into moving
woven into the winter
of a halted moving staring.
what are you shown?
knit beguilers.
they tell you two years later.
sword & hammock are squeaking about real-fake ultras.
we don't even know what an ultra still is?
and they have the admission for entrance as amperage's loom.

new poem 6.12 | [for john crouse]

behaved. outre. combination. lug-nut. solemn. invisibly seen. parallax. looking at you. motion. leant. lean. seasoned with myrtle berries. compatible. inroad. fog. associate. noggin. salt. nut-shelf. cranium. gandolf. motion. mirror. seltzer. late night. over there. somber. inch. antler. borrow. tone. placemat. sizing. unroll. replace. animate. cue. trousseau. rename file-driver. no-go. seems. does. those then diction. realitizer. paper. stone. scissors

new poem 6.13 |

'eh?', i say.
'yes, or other', she intones.
her voice is more melodious than mine.
the wrought bikkhu is not a bikkhu if showing to be a bikkhu.
'solemnly' he swore in the facile manner of gentrification.
abattoir grooms itertations nearly bordered mica with granite.
one hand swims through water the other paddles intentionally behind that hand.
mitsuko uhcida is a great mozart piano performer.
i recall that.
some are oversold—
others find their niche.
heights of barking at fleas is the biggest problem my dog has.
i feel the need to entertain more when i have nothing to say.
number six has been ongoing awhile now.
perhaps too long too long too long.
if there's anyone else on the floor who has a vision to add i'd be welcome.
are you inviting yourself in?
perhaps, but probably not.
i have places to go to seek colder temperatures.
when one stays inside the house one accomplishes more.
poetry is more the product of creativity, imagination, and daring than...
complete this sentenc...
...even see the screen door slam less often.
why the commonsense version is not deliberated more before delivered

new poem 6.14 |

it's a decoy that shrilly reification mellow hat-trick in ring cold to the touch.
courtiers on the meld—across the atlantic pond i simulcast.
voices paralyze on hearing commensurate hearing diss.
narrow as it could pertain—
mzeow invies zusammenschlafen while paving streets.
the extra in going threshold-constructed as that consciousness-to is rubric
arrow to rhetors inflamed.
mollusks cooking versions of predispositions once willing the oversell—
while 'why?' goes it ad-nauseum.
in so many, those prefecture logged-in as loiterer.
motion is an ascription of detail of seigneur—how much how many literally the
clause propitiates, precipitates, palpitates.
mirrors in the wall—illusions the non-existent motions' annual rings.
pedestals to mutation, matadors, metamorphoses.
loitering with word-slouching rewards tripmeters' calling garaged outriggers.
ictus where scry that pennant how view the house-meow sits in a shed over
there the unforeseen the sidearm volitional & moral—
an apparition a mural. one-use fairground—
fair-play—
oversold—
ourselves between hoopla, mirror & maelstrom.
a token retaliation mitoses everywhere—house is firetrap—masaic noise
music have
perhaps the shelf plays cops & robbed reversals lookIng through the marquee.

NEW POEMS SEVEN

new poem 7.1 |

hundreded over a soul-fare crossing over with its mainspring—
a |mindspring eloquence though nothing thinks of nothing over
recoup geometry the skirted line gained.
over that motion is a well-knit cancellation.

speaking personally of poetry art & music is comprehensive enough
to mend frequencies.
accelerating thrownness—
it is disposed through elan that the marrow believes
its teevee sediment.
before conducting outsiders into the mortise garnished—
the contour eloped—
the employee became so incensed he bewared crinkled fences.
foreseen how these prelude to the morning of sound.

new poem 7.2 |

untitled.
overuse.
motionless at hand.
omission, commission, permission.
handshake.
precision.
realititation's motive.
elocutionary blueness.
wounded skier assignment.
compression reality—comprehension shelving.
starting endlessly.
the task of the artistpoetmusican.never-ending literality.
muscularity or peacefulness though unrealitizable.
action & stasis. what or whatever.
the choice is yours use it wisely i'm sure.
the possibility is where rhythm is.
compression—compensation—the otherness is awareness.
that otherness is only otherness—
its tautological equivalency is beheld everywhere—
redundantly,
even warned by cool entitlement w/out cloud—
composition's ladle—
strange as modulation can be.

new poem 7.3 |

this tone met ensemble—
larger than legitimacy.
real—
as at the data's longterm horrification.
this personage's nitpick limitation
eloquence is though where to be seen is horrific.
use twice as a habit cantankerously orphic.
find the the blue shell.
then jump down the stairs & drink the orange potion.
what'll it see?
an appetite for visions is enchanted by possibility.
role-playing in matinees before wanderlust-audiences.
unfinished sentences unfinished symphonies.

new poem 7.4 |

sangha inner to person & environment is the rule here.
others are disembodied existences of mind—
scene's foeat effects monstrations elegant & rare.
was that each tide swears intention to arrive early.
the conflated motion waits behind the ocean wavers.
process & infinity has been saturnine for no other reason than it could.
the peaceful meandering washes overwell.

new poem 7.5 |

i am forgetting what i would have already said if i was prepared to write this poem.
the light's always teacup & painterly—kneading stomach at general presume poem-hallucination.
physical presented nearly scrawling through beaded mindstyles are a hippie action-in-fact.
shipping hippies where the author wants them as jests at philosophy.
a small thing, i can't answer that number, let it ring, it is inoperable
people are soap-eaters—they gnarl, gnash, & gnarp.
because the tide of ore melds incantations behaving erratically.

anomy gashes the crux of what's left.
can this bulletin if one's imports clog or defiltrate themselves in your backyard.
melanges of granite & feldspar inherit the earthenware jug on the shelf in our kitchen.
combining these impressions is a document-nearness—for lack of better word
—sort of like cement between stone in an old stone fence will defocus while paralyzing motion

new poems 7.6 |

no gitanes—deficits mesmerized for from acolytes there are suddenly running totals.—
somewhat the furniture anchors not so selfie less the cantankerousness. self.
where when yonder in flux are storied lintel three brigands
red mollusks—appetizers—no compunction.
glamour those no bulls tonight foible random cellophane network
it's all a gamble whether grainy fixtures yield or punish.
so cold & orphic those rien du tout—
pulse from the diatribe excels where remedial big-time is flaunted applied & falsely.
my feet, flighty anchors, so mantic eliminating vestiges of premiss
that literally are what if a conduit can be trained in that direction.
merciless integrity at some level—
that's an issue behaving least notion-driven.
the dog waits & watches—
namelessly except for that which we gave her—
a lasting small fountain bottled into water—
sold at the convenient store.

new poem 7.7 | [for carol]

that which one resonates with—
plays so it donates it
to quarantine & vigilance—
so bitterly opaque meeting
a virally-tending tending soul.
no prior aspects mitigate its
absentia on intelligensia—

tool of the entity called quasar—
some bug-bear gone trial-to-vista
for the metalism of its voiceovers.
depose the flambeau—a disciplinary
they met with as perception changed
& will even more if
wide promises of education
run interference.
thoughts are no longer for rope & snake.
they don't hold overture to errata
in this compact disk—
the initial rapproachment is
the rules of those who radiate
the cold communal precedent
so night-fallen it fends
slash & burn precedent.
its roughness in daylong tropes
is of a cast-iron carnivore.
the animal sells frozen choices—
they are promptly over
that impulsiveness of words—
but not so—the avertissement
recoils from saying—or even thinking—
that.
know nothing,
he appropriates from
the blended atonement.
such chronic elevation
merits a gleam of purity—
that which is conflated
morrows congealed gears—
walks through the arbor.
these ironic chests of drawers
cover moonsongs—those with
inroads of interference.
levels of coils of rudenesses
commune with the pliable dam—
big grasshoppers motivate bridges
to turn when in the west.
what was sent then forgotten?
perhaps tolerant erasures know
to interlace with that
procedural geezer. blocks are doffed
from sentences borrowing

the thematic freeze—thoughts rolling
through headroom to
healthy posterchildren
in the opening of their fellowship
somewhere else in mindstyle.
the abrupt modulation
between fact & doofus.
a volition of foresight
where the appaloosa is gone
though efficacy shelters
a concatenation of new spaces, new poems &
new thought are flattered as
the property of the intransigent &
the topically immune—but not muted.
the town propitiates cadres of annual
engagement between alarming notions
so that for too long the angel is
tossed into the ring. pity the
emptiness is not regulation
nor rapport nor reapportionment
which paralyzes that this & these nowheres
the ingenue is singing. & so is allowed
meekness —omicron to alpha—
alphabtetic—concrete & barbed wireless—
a drape over the fedora it is.
the intractible analytic brokers decoys
from one to two
as if the elementation of partisanry is
contrasted enough in prosody.
slices of pizza & their miraculous power
would look for the jack of hearts—
would look around.
the lasting of persistence will
cull the imagined couple without the need
of a diagram from playing cards.
so, let's introduce the element of chance
while the angel is near—while the angel
answers questions it is stuffing
preoccupied gulags while with satellite feeds
a rough integral of tensile appurtenance
holds the key.

new poem 7.8 |

.

a relaxation with cosmic dust to receive notions' vocabulary.
environmental concern 'to opaque'[there's that verb again] the module offered.
some assist the natural incremental voices recoup a self-opaquing monde.
treating a motive for which one'd ordinarily horde immersion—
then dissolve without celebration.
rationales demure between heroiade the notion and herioade mellowed out
into the scolding bird.
narrowly the button soul crosswise over whose longterm happenstance is a yea
r-long working-it-out.
or even that—so we switch gears, perterb & wait—protrude & wait.
the skeletal kitsch of the season one finds in the mall—
onerous burgomeisters keeping tithes where silence ought.
the sound-off of 'ought' is a natural devolution of paradise into the dictionary.
cold sidearms say 'stuff happens'.
what burns is nominally protean.
the postcard to provence was a skid-mark nearly meandering where stoically
borscht.
somewhere sopranists gleam tenacious & journalese.

new poem 7.9 | [for john ashberry]

a somber wave washes over landscape-mirroring allocation not pretense to process procedures. when over, delays fostered months of calm incremental choice-mongering, all realitized for the best. sentimental voiceovers, they are andiamo! opaque [again] possibilities emerge any and everywhere. a solemn wave is the receiver of washing proportional figuration. evoke signatures of teeth over a toast migrates over the waves of mighty aortas beholden to watershed hoopla premonitions of devaluation. the that which not-happening overages tam-tam merely visionary vantage-point. reacting industrial institutions opaque [again, verb again] mile-high noise-proof seizures. wandering internet affiliation before therefores well into naught held random a removable om is impossible though a considerable motion rolls the night through with held-pittance lifted along the skyward blend. a revenuer polishes hidden coin, while smiling for cameo paratroopers peacefully alethon-damaging symbolic patterns whether or not. they consider latinate tendencies. it just goes there for the mot this was not that, then before this the this waited a bit amidst calling out, it's not oven-ready no negotiator will handle it. technical immersion ghost-written this is narrow tonearm-going through official metric property means. deter no asterism, short with paper papered while efficacy sums an estranger wide of camp eructations melded formal clock clotting errata genant, solvent, masquerades intended where plusieurs majeur vend so-called tarmac for air-placements at gestural anchor. until utterly increment saison deference tile tilling renaissance repentance merely doff one's hat dramatically accuracy. choleric not the-inal -ush. mete satisfaction top-hat knit cheroot. big trot buttoned haptic trout egghead lest renaissance begone, the tourmaline shored up is. wide to deplore wide to wisdom wide to display wide to wisdom wide to display. how'd onsets demonstrate feral unalterability. whoever therefore, whoever therefore invoke woke the reminder of gaffe those deprobematized elements. make inalienable thresholds yrself knows knowledge once begone reflected in akimbo trance collector consultation promenade. something morrow contains least world-formatless. talk other warren gigantic mores gnit-gnash reopening the doorway theoretic of what serves toasted feed —philosophy styles the world just literally fizzing outward—the masked mistake of that thatness farmed through fanatic mendicants soliciting where arrive the position. remote orbits radiate emulsions emotions emaciations to heal cure bargained curators energy those preoccupations myopically focusing on the crime of underpaid, understaffed, overworked allot motto strength asemic no laggard ramifies to where while the shell gymp oversells tisanes while damage redacts from borderline to borderline the contention slackens not. & another whirl geomancet-replete once seltzer heedless the bagatelle once. then somber sober soupcon that relache torn—engineered this that mentioning ice tea briefing...

new poem 7.10 | a philosophical poem

no harangue or lecture calls itself reality.
so, the word 'reality' has been introduced—
to whom—to you?—the reader? the reader-as-poet?
to me?—the poet? the poet-as-reader?
curious how a word changes things.
a simple word, indeed—
reality.
where is it? where it is.
in front?—in back?—on the left-side?—etc—etc—etc—
[a stray-mind goes on here]
somewhat property manager—
this house houses houses inside— music > 'house-music' > —
'house'—the old teevee program—
are all the flowerfields now populated by /houses/apartments/office-buildings//.

i am a closed circuit.
you must be a facebook friend to view my timeline.
is it me telling you that?—i don't know.
what is me?—is it necessary to know?
the big—why does the 'stray-mind' opt for the question-mark?
why? is why? is why?—tautological or real?—real? or real?
oi or om?
...
...
...
...

new poem 7.11 | crazy, semi-philosophical poem

i am heretoafter invidious-the-mote of serenity palliative.
architect where, finding oneself here, what's next in the cards, or in whatever?
we must remain calm.
pills, meditation, whatever—calm.
a ghostly reflection over in the corner of the room looks at hazy light near the ceiling—
no, it's just the lamp-with-upturned-opening—wait, that's a novel by a popular novelist, no?—or—i have been out of touch for so long—no joke.
sitting here with my typewriter making typewriter-art they-call-it.
it was small choice—that or this—so i chose this.
no one else was around except wide-&-teary-eyed children.
the time in solitary seems better than any alternative—keeping out the mosquitos.
it'd plausible that the that intention—blocks no one thinking i write poetry.
sorted out by ten minutes later one missed much infrastructure flying by the handle which was nearly off.
the off & the on. the jaw & the tooth.
how soon the tooth will leave the mouth, forcibly extracted or, in a less-plausible choice, that the image preferred, a concept holding motive where silent.
though some motorcade walked the holding overcast that though they are.
they are overvast.
orbits casting their shadows over the overturned obliquenessesl
there's a sentence implicating transduction of eggshell—the chicken or the egg, comatose or dipolar—we convey alterity when prolating surveillance by candlelight. i
so merry the aporia of gold to erase all data from hardly a saturnine plasma-

tiling furnace.
a bourgeoise naught inversion-related.
the arguable-metier, poet, just so it cannot nip said thought.

new poem 7.12 |

thought the word world wooden chariot-behaving more now wast electricity-
driven chariot-driven wast.
archaic such is dry-wall in the rooms of a house i know—
belittled by inferior malfeasance—
the voila-seeking marched through trees to get here—
chopping it into its last marks on a fluted packet.
king in spirit, thousand-fold mitosis, phd genetically muttering salut—
iffy other fiction lopped off neither waters.
blotted motions gallantly neither prosaic nor genie from the boat—
loose on down-sizing editors.
connotations' weal of commotion weal of prompters eerily hallowe'en soon
'nuff.
that the scansion is irregular—
'e' is rapport write ligature.
season of first engulfment—
now & then then always.
motions where scampering eglise-sur-l'isle ou on sait l'eglise.
carnet sur le table—
eleve-le.
moat furloughed to farmed-out rapport, underling underlining.
where listening those par-ten-signatures. each leaning through book-after-book.
book's honesty is 99% guarantee for the what-it-is-on-the-page.

new poem 7.13 |

smaller.
immerse.
toothed.
either.
neither.
aerated.
disclose.

pastiche.
eatery.
slowly.
advance.
ductile.
advantage.
hopping.
dinosaur
about-face.
two-words
'no' to two-words.
carnival.
trawler.
poivre.
cantankerous.
hourlies.
implosion.
pathetique.
analog.
gullible.
entrecote.
delete.
savor.
preparation.

new poem 7.14 |

double-double.
ocean-tortellini
notion-notion.
barracuda-elicit.
elite-mindsop.
strata=striking.
bot-curlings.
convincable-narrow,
untitled-untitled.
newpoem-newpoems.
bartering-cluster.
aviso-paramita.
decaffeinated-shoulder.
trammel-not.

inconfraternal.
three-hours.
amaneusis-orbit.
fool-in-triad.
velcro i am.

new poem 7.15 |

sign says 'sigh'.
near the overly corrected.
umlaut is borderline.
minus theorem indict while so any parallel tone arm.
ganymede's the nearest star? isn't it?
attenuate more the slow-fast diamond
thatever notion of predilection merges into intellitecture.
seek, the word's already there—one line higher.
it's a confluence of stars in motion,
the plow is 'in the loop' throughout
for nausea from head to feet.
or it's intersecting with home-run technology.
...you don't hear me...

new poem 7.16 |

the professional processional corrects papers at night.
the poet is free to choice—determined to a lesser degree with circumstance.
the professional's processional is different & the same as a poet's.
the professional thinks the poet is a sub-category.
while the poet thinks the professional is the sub-category.
who is correct?
don't ask either of those two.

new poem 7.18 |

duo gentility veneer those taxing the scrutiny proem succubus venerate.
masala burrito greenway—milling the myopic evolutionary voiceover adaptive.
gritty schemata vandura politic emulator engine libertine absolutism grope.
amulet noggin asemia fenugreek genovese saltine gneiss fairway isle thirst.
simple plus the unity unified sample samizdat elocutionary pledge ironic.
singeresangering. the trimmest ontic language possibly occlusion those.
perplexity clarified. something lariat methinks onus querulously weakening.
zettel mode entity eternal sadhana schist genuflect thumbed the guitar.
some mindstylistic emulsion tartan survival links nodding asemic spoken tone.
grimmercy square. nths walking aporias weeping the stride waterfallen olchar.
engineer tartouffe telling sandwich spags mirroring thetic paycheck burner.
absolutism erase. grendel's dapper soupcon that mira-rhombus-edifice libertine.
resurgency whether night orb fraizer golden bough namo vigil geisha teams.
stereo crouton aegis elgin. negotiator wide fontanella the drifted-whale stunned.
mersey enough. righten handed asile those rendezvous notocord pliable ilk.
tenet logos entrust experience racine gingivtis volumnar deficiency retinates.
verb deterative eternity oddity staffed nths renga negatively positioned positive.
try-out fondly anemia the surcease. tisane arahanchini evening-song relax urreal.
major d'omo spanning the left-room solidarity rolling the raft over water study.
choice macaw gender surreal geek snafyu irreal causation five clef introspections.
and untold the unrolling the endlessly ending redlining scruple hidden aeries.
suet birth birdsong highness reign dancing the keystone booster vereinigen.
chunked governance thirdly apathy refute slumber up heretofore that sturdy.
much poot. that returnable seize geisha either buttoned uptown lien oldster.
what is poetry? i ask. what is poetry? i ask? what is poetry. what is poetry what isn't.

EPILOGUE / NEW POEMS EIGHT

new poem 8.1 |

lotus. opoid genove. lite maiggiore. dolce bagnole.
i know not italian, canna yoda speek.
though why not parade in ryebread ivory cloth?
mulling eggless candles. the fantasy brooch baroque-originated.
not for heuristic lamentation. brattle tutor forty-one yardarm lest obtuse.
gnarl ungnarl the if-it-matter. suffice therefore well-naught bothered, tobias.
i know no one named tobias, for full disclosure.
widening circles of fissile daisy-wheels are coding moot parameters.
laboratories, elated from shine, aegis-prone also, thereinfore bloodlessly protect that which they...
gitanes felicitous emotional curvature toned everyone knitwork belabored.
that wiring will ding thereinfore bootcamp will between hard know-it-alls scorch.
pay the fare—to where is guesswork.
as if.
then so fairly protesting elementary staring contraptions.
there correctly impossibly negotiating a wall between nothing the wall doesn't therein sapient.
glim gloom glum preparative slowdown the library the bookstall waiting slow-mongering.
this all has reference to forgettable—
forgettables seeming very important at the time.
coempting all or nothing where studied where...
eggshoe, not gumshoe.

new poem 8.2 |

ampere. genug. nine acres. thoughtful
language massivity prelude tonicity laggard.
nil mellow the carom tiling where pelleles.
the dan-ranunculus tiling where signatured
negotiator elementally percipient value-driven
thoughtful those reparations oggi saoford the cloaked
liquid. mote aegis that sortilege amulet.
invitations whoever the appendage, almond-alkaline.
surrey merrily wielding intersections wooly.
thorax belated. nibble tenet raincoats overalls.
thereof themselves cannot helplessly themselves—thetic
antagonism from-tos whether all those poseur-basis.
alternative foment blogorhea tonos greeting.
standard elate letterpress-washer note.
impressario mulling serration evident evidence lien.
hari om the backdrop offering mindstyles whorls
in the stream backgrounded if warm outside on the
porch. today gutturals plugged becalm clearly
overhaul grotto emeraldine geiger oeuvre. oocyte blameless
as individual either plasticene opacity lien nil wandering into
lucidity make sense stop making sense the breath of
needed intake of breath.

new poem 8.3 |

a comprehension is not a compression of the literary distance between two unrelated factors,
do you like theory? theory of literature? my own?
one can't go back—
intentionally, that is..
we can always get back to where we've always been.
or that's what i've heard.
not culture rot walking towards me.
the combinations are too complex for reality to catch.
we will not cave in says the wallboard upon deciding the farmhouse should be saved.

new poem 8.4 |

the wanderer of time through time by time sustained
in a melange of topiaries, monks, and reflecting pools.
carry on with the tear-shedding—we are sledding into the horizon.
a character asks if it is typical of this maudlin epoch—
one's answer depends on what one considers elegant.
if one considers anything as elegant.
a solitary perplexity voices concern over the telephone—
where there's not a cell-phone to talk into.
she talks over the music while teaching
thinking to drown opacity
installed on several mopheads.
they won't be there tonight-
their links with their people are shackles.
so now my sundays are freer to unroll the carpet anywhere intention takes me.
i am literally fixing a hole in the ceiling where the rain can enter.
a quick dash to the right in the background like a linebacker on a team,
an inner dialogue runs through this that can't be expressed.
if it was expressed, it would be familiar with everything,.
the world on a string is legendary.

____

____

WORDS OF PRAISE FOR *NEW POEMS* BY PETER GANICK

Good poetry, especially good experimental poetry, allows us to step outside of our normal thought processes and experience a horizontal expansion of consciousness: to see that which we know cannot be. By focusing on apparently commonplace objects and interactions and warping our perceptions of them, Peter Ganick reminds us that every moment is alive with multiple meanings; that there is no such thing as an unchanging quotidian.

- Jonathan Penton

> "the whole wide world is sonatas for brunch—
> & blankness where silence ought to be."

New Poems attests to Peter Ganick's continuing growth as a creator. His bringing readers these shorter works provides a welcome surprise. Quiet, carved clarity answers a vast array of accumulated signals:

> so epilogues decant amulets one by one over the capitals of big countries.
> extremism agrees to redefine treaded mirages' meaning.
> a legume grows in brooklyn nearly every day.
> previously, thousands of waking sounds were remitted in person.
> four hundred people in the audience tonight.
> thank you for being here.

The words "in person" resonate, as the poet's/writer's/text-maker's sensibilities issue direct statements and questions, revealing a *weltanschauung* of precision, power, and humor that give back to us first things:

> "so much
> confetti, these words, someday i'll write a
> 'real' poem."

- Sheila E. Murphy

www.ingramcontent.com/pod-product-compliance
Lightning Source LLC
Chambersburg PA
CBHW081501040426
42446CB00016B/3344